Missing Impossible

Missing Impossible

Trevillion's Method of Perfect Putting

PAUL TREVILLION

PELHAM BOOKS

PELHAM BOOKS

Published by the Penguin Group
27 Wrights Lane, London w8 5TZ
Viking Penguin Inc., 375 Hudson Street, New York, New York 10014, USA
Penguin Books Australia Ltd, Ringwood, Victoria, Australia
Penguin Books Canada Ltd, 10 Alcorn Avenue, Toronto, Ontario, Canada M4V 3B2
Penguin Books (NZ) Ltd, 182–190 Wairau Road, Auckland 10, New Zealand

Penguin Books Ltd, Registered Offices: Harmondsworth, Middlesex, England

First published in Great Britain 1996

Copyright © Paul Trevillion 1996

The original edition of this book was published as
The Perfect Putting Method by Paul Trevillion
by Pelham Books in 1971

Typeset in 12/15pt Monophoto Garamond by Selwood Systems Ltd, Midsomer Norton
Printed in England by Butler & Tanner Limited, Frome and London

A CIP catalogue record for this book is available from the British Library

ISBN 0 7207 2060 5

The moral right of the author has been asserted

Contents

CONTENTS

Part One

INTRODUCTION

It's easy, so easy, to miss a short four-foot putt. They all do it – your heroes, my heroes, you! – but not me. I don't miss. In fact I haven't missed from four feet for nearly thirty years, but I'll come to that later.

It's a well known fact that if a golfer misses a putt from four feet it's down to the golfer, there are no excuses.

The story goes that, in 1957 at the Eastern Open Championship, American Tommy Bolt was asked by the press whether or not he was satisfied with his putting. Tommy thought for a moment, scratching his long, lean jaw, and said, 'If I made every putt for the rest of my life I still wouldn't be even.'

Today Tom Watson is saying pretty much the same. The truth is, Tom Watson is hitting the ball from tee to green in major championships better than when he was winning a hatful of titles, but he can't get the ball to disappear from sight with one touch of his putter when he is on the green, putter-length away from the hole.

Now ask yourself, why should that be?

Even the legendary golfer Gene Sarazen, at the age of ninety-three, can hit the opening drive at the Masters tournament in front of thousands of paying customers and multi-media hype and split the centre of the fairway; and yet on the best-prepared surface of the course, from a laughable four feet, he can't guarantee to knock the ball in the hole.

So what's the answer? No one has put it better than Dr Garfield Evans, of Cathedral Road, Cardiff, Wales.

Evans would rest a putter head on the ground as close as possible to the ball with the blade meticulously at right angles to the line of flight. Leaving the putter head completely at rest, he moved behind the ball and with his right foot gave the putter head a gentle kick. The ball went straight into the hole. Said the doctor,

It proves a point that the larger muscles in the body, the leg muscles in this case, can withstand stress to a far greater degree than the smaller muscles in the wrists. Notice when a person gets nervous how it is the hands that are the first to tremble. It would need an earth-shattering shock, far bigger than one would experience in golf, to get a man shaking from head to foot.

The doctor was right. The large muscles in the body can withstand pressure. That's why I grip the putter with my left hand at the top of the shaft, extend my right hand down the shaft, and in doing so eliminate my wrists from the action and execute the stroke with my right shoulder.

For close on thirty years I have preached this method.

Today Bernhard Langer with a 'mirror image' of my split-hand method, has won many titles, including the US Masters. Sam Torrance, Mark James, Philip Walton and Peter Senior are picking up titles almost every week with their Broom Handles and split-hand putting technique ... but I'm racing ahead of myself.

The 1990s have seen an explosion of top professionals from around the world turning to various forms of split-hand putting.

From the American tour, Bruce Lietzke, Rocco Mediate, John Adams, Mark Lye, Keith Fergus and Hal Sutton have all split the hands. In the US the words 'split-hand grip' are now firmly entrenched in American golf terminology. The commentators repeatedly refer to it when describing the revolution in the putting grip.

Australians have had a particularly successful time with it. Peter Senior's career has gone upwards in a big way and both Brett Ogle and Wayne Riley are members of the split-hand group.

Then from Europe we have Bernhard Langer, Sam Torrance, Mark James, Philip Walton and Tommy Horton.

Truly, it can be said that split-hand putting is a world-wide phenomenon.

Because of the many championships these split-hand golfers were winning, people began to seek me out, referring back to my book *The Perfect Putting Method*, published in 1971 by Pelham Books and out of print, asking my opinion on why split-hand putting works.

So I have decided to update my book and explain the

secret which I have formulated and updated over the last thirty-odd years.

Let's start at the very beginning. The year 1968 and the four-foot miss that changed my life.

Chapter 1

The Four-foot Miss that Changed my Life

It was a simple, no borrow, four-foot putt. All I had to do for an eagle was knock the ball in the hole. I can recall now how I set myself over the putt and stroked the ball towards the hole. It was on line and dead centre of the hole. But as I straightened up I knew it wasn't going to drop, and it didn't. It stopped a good three inches short. For a moment I stood there looking at it, I was so annoyed I was numb. A few minutes before I had just hit two perfect golf shots – the first a drive of a little over 200 yards which had comfortably cleared the river on the par-5 15th at Enfield Golf Club. The ball came to rest in the middle of the fairway, I was able to take a 3-wood for my second shot. I hit the ball well. It sailed over the hill where, to my joy, it rolled down over the dry hard fairway and onto the green, coming to rest no more than four feet from the hole. Having never reached this green in two before I was, for the first time, putting for an eagle. There was no way I could miss the putt – but I did. How? Even today I still do not know.

Having missed, I decided not to putt out for a 4. I simply walked up and knocked the ball off the green. In my anger I hit the ball hard, very hard and it disappeared into some rough at the side of the green. I kept on walking, I didn't even bother to look for it. I climbed up on to the 16th tee and hit two consecutive drives into the out-of-bounds on the right. They proved to be the last two golf shots to be hit by me on a golf course for over a year. I rammed my driver deep into the golf bag and stormed off.

On the drive home I replayed the putt a dozen times and, of course, the ball always dropped – but what was the point? In two strokes I had covered, to perfection, 453 yards only to be cheated by the last four feet. It seemed so pointless that so much good play could be undone by a few miserable feet on the green. It was no comfort admitting that everybody misses their share of short putts – why should they? Ask yourself, what would a professional do if, from the tee he only hit a handful of fairways during a round. The answer is obvious, he would take his swing to pieces. Yet, I have seen golfers – professional golfers – take 35–40 putts a round, failing to register a single one-putt green because they missed from within the four-foot mark more times than I guess they would care to admit. And yet, strangely enough, they accept it, assured by the thought that the putts will drop tomorrow – but, of course, as we all know they never do. And yet these same golfers will, if they have missed two greens with their approach shots, go out and practise at length that department of their game.

Ask a professional why he is not out there on the

putting green endeavouring to perfect his putting stroke and he will, as likely as not, tell you 'You've got to be a born putter. No amount of practising will make you one, it's all in the mind.' Truth is that hot summer I believed the same, I had been missing more than my share of short putts. The fun had gone out of the game. Hell, if you can't sink the putts, what's the point of getting the ball on the green in the first place? So I decided to give up the game, and I did. I have never played a serious round of golf since.

Chapter 2
Joe Davis Shows the Way

Although I had stopped playing the game of golf, I couldn't stop thinking about it. Why should putting be so difficult, not only for myself but for every class of golfer? I refused to accept the theory that good putters are born. Such a doctrine didn't hold water. There was nothing difficult about knocking a ball along the ground, it required no special gifts of nature – a child could do it. No, nearer the truth was that golfers in general spent 90 per cent of their time on practising the shots that were to get them on the green. Only a grudging 10 per cent was allocated to practising their putting. Little wonder that tournament professionals never completely master the simple art of putting.

Strange as it may seem, I was inspired to take out my putter again after watching the top snooker champions in action. Since that day in 1955 when Joe Davis registered his crowning achievement – snooker's maximum break of 147 (15 reds, 15 blacks and all the colours) – I had always taken a great interest in snooker. Possibly this is why I had never accepted the argument that putting brings about numerous mental pressures because of the time factor involved. Agreed, in football, tennis, rugby, etc., the mental pressures are slightly less for here the ball is played to you and you react instinctively. Nevertheless in comparable sports to golf – snooker, archery and shooting, for example – one has to propel the object to the target from a stationary position, and it is very rare indeed for one of these sportsmen to suffer from the dreaded 'shakes' which for one reason or another attacks many world class players when they step on to the putting surface.

When watching Joe Davis play I always formed the opinion that it was a far tougher proposition to knock a snooker ball into the pocket from ten feet than it is to knock a perfectly straight putt in from four feet. I am sure you will agree that the mental pressures in all world class sports are uniform and yet I never once saw Joe Davis attempt to lag up when ten feet from the pocket. This, of course, is one of the secrets why snooker players and the like do not suffer from the 'yips'. Every time they line up the ball – and, remember, they sometimes have to knock it in off two cushions, every bit as difficult as negotiating a borrow on the green – they have a positive attitude.

They are concentrating on one thing, ball to pocket. Striving for perfection with every stroke teaches snooker players to live with and overcome pressure. This is why Arnold Palmer in his heyday was, by far, the best putter I have ever seen. He always went for the hole.

At all times, the snooker player, the archer, the marksman aim for perfection – they have to if they are

Arnold Palmer

to score well. Not so the golfer – the truth is, golf is a game which allows for too great a margin for error. Only on the putting green do the golfers strive for absolute perfection. Possibly this is why only on the putting green the pressure affects them.

From the tee he can be as much as twenty feet off line and still be on the fairway. His approach shot can be twenty feet from the flag and it is still on the green. Both shots will receive generous applause from the gallery. He can then lag his twenty-foot putt two feet short and receive even greater applause. In no other sport can such a margin of error receive such high appraisal. A bowler at cricket need be no more than eight inches off line to miss the wicket. A batsman's error of judgement can be as little as two inches and he will snick a possible catch. The prize fighter has to be no more than a sixteenth of an inch out to miss his opponent altogether.

Possibly a better example is the juggler on the stage – how many times have you seen one of these performers put a spoon on the toe of his shoe, flick it up eight feet in the air and land it in a cup balanced on his head? Such a variety artiste can do this time after time. He can do this because he has a positive thought action, he allows no margin for error. Unlike the golfer, he has no thoughts of lagging up, the spoon must drop into the cup every time.

Here was the answer. Golfers, especially on the green, apply only part of their concentration to knocking the ball in the hole. The mechanics of the swing dominates their thoughts, at least 90 per cent of their concentration

is applied to keeping their head and body still, taking the putter back square to the hole, accelerating through the ball and then following through square to the hole.

THE SNOOKER PLAYER CONCENTRATES ON WHERE HE IS GOING TO HIT THE BALL, THE GOLFER CONCENTRATES ON HOW HE IS GOING TO HIT IT.

I am quite sure I am right here, more so after seeing Joe Davis at a pro-am golf tournament. Davis, faced with a four-foot putt, lay full stretch on the green and knocked the ball in using the handle-end of the putter exactly like a cue. Two holes later he had another four-foot putt. I thought he was going to repeat his snooker act. Instead, he lined it up like a tournament professional, went through his pre putting drill – then he missed. Davis had fallen for the four-card trick.

The first stage of my new putting stroke was to split my hands on the club, the same way a snooker player splits his hands on the cue. A right-handed snooker player steadies the cue with his left hand and hits the ball with his right – thinking ball-to-pocket. I copied. I steadied the putter with the left hand, extended my right hand down the shaft and concentrated on just knocking the ball into the hole, using my right hand only. I thought of only one thing – ball-to-hole. I practised this way with every length of putt from two feet to twenty feet. I was after perfection and since that day I have never lagged a putt.

Chapter 3

I Become the World's Greatest Putter

Splitting my hands on the golf club and striking the ball with my right hand only, meant I was now dropping a great deal of putts, but not all. If I was to become infallible from four feet and under I would have to search still further for the perfect method.

American Phil Rodgers had been using a split-hand putting grip taught to him by Paul Runyan – he, too, missed putts. In fact, Bob Charles, the tall slim New Zealander, using the orthodox putting grip, completely out-played Rodgers on the greens when he won the British Open in 1963. In the two extra rounds of the play-off for the Championship, Charles took a total of 57 putts to Rodgers's 65 – an eight-shot difference, precisely the margin of Charles's victory.

I began to search through Runyan's theories, he had made a mistake somewhere. If I was to improve I had to find it. Apparently Runyan turned to splitting his hands on the golf club thirty years ago when competing in the Belmont Open in Boston. Heavy winds had begun to affect his putting. In seeking a method to stabilise himself he anchored the butt-end of the shaft against his waist, gripped tightly with the left hand at the top and extended the right hand down the back side of the shaft.

He was so encouraged by the results that after the tournament he decided to test it thoroughly. From two feet either side of the hole he checked how many putts he could sink before missing. The top figure for the old method was 143, for the new style 400.

Unfortunately Runyan discovered that the split-hand method had a distinct disadvantage on the longer putts. His swing arc was limited by his ANCHORED left hand which gripped the top of the shaft. So Runyan, instead of making his left wrist work like a HINGE, decided to use a longer putter and this, I discovered, was where he made his fatal error. Runyan, one step from perfection, had overlooked the obvious. The reason he was sinking so many putts the old way was because he dropped the right hand down the shaft and got it near to the point of action – the putter blade. Furthermore he got his eyes right down over the ball. In other words, the DISTANCE problem was halved by his former exaggerated bending from the waist.

Like the top croquet players, he had reduced the amount of footage to be negotiated. That footage being eyes-to-ball, ball-to-hole. As you can see from the illustration on page 18, I have practically half the problem facing Runyan when sinking a three-foot putt. Using a longer shaft, Runyan pushed his eyes up too far from the ball and further increased his problem of distance.

Like Runyan, I too decided that the standard putter

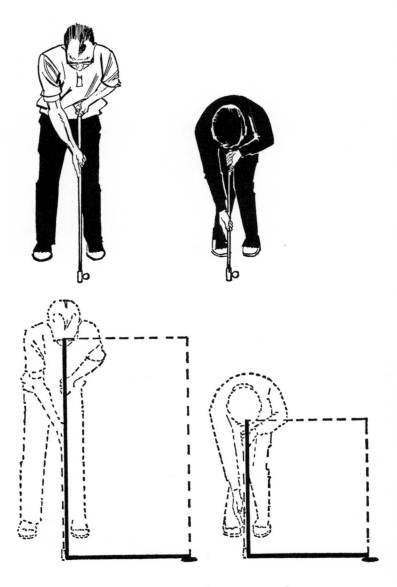

Runyan-Trevillion putting styles compared

needed to be modified but I worked in the opposite direction to Runyan. I cut five inches off the length of my putter. I was now like the snooker player, right down over the ball. I could feel the strike of the putt in my right hand and the confidence this gave me when holing out was immeasurable.

The first day I stepped on to the practice green with my short putter I holed 538 four-foot putts before missing. Fired with my success I set myself the target of sinking 1,000 four-foot putts consecutively. I was one day short of two weeks achieving this goal. Twice during this time I got into the magic 900s and failed. This was the testing time for I began to question that, perhaps, even this method collapsed under pressure. But, once

having reached the elusive 1,000 mark, I knew I had found the secret for I never missed again.

At first I found it hard to believe that every four-foot putt would drop but as the days passed I learned to accept my invincibility. I was infallible and two years later, January 1970, I wrote about my findings in *Golf Illustrated*. By this time I had sunk countless thousands of four-foot putts without missing once. In that same period of time not one world class golfer came within an ocean of my achievement ... Archer, Charles, Player, Palmer and Casper, all the world's great putters, had missed their share of four-footers during that time.

I claimed in print that I could beat them all and I issued a challenge to every golfer in the world. The stake – £1,000 upwards. The distance from the hole – four feet. I knew I could beat all-comers so I sat back and waited for the chance to prove it.

Chapter 4

The Challengers Came – We Putted – I Conquered

My challenge did not go unheeded, letters poured into the *Golf Illustrated* offices, my telephone did not stop ringing, one man even travelled all the way down from Scotland with a £200 challenge. *Golf Illustrated* gave it front-page coverage and this is the story they carried on 29 January 1970:

THE PUTTS ARE DROPPING!
TREVILLION UNDEFEATED – WINS £200 ON ONE PUTT AND GIVES IT TO CHARITY.
Peter Willis reports
The signs indicate that the Trevillion putting method for four-footers and under, publicised in this magazine last week, will be seen in force on the golf courses this Spring. Initial reaction from club golfers who have tried the split-hand method is that it works!

Trevillion, who has now stepped up his daily practice to a minimum of 1,000 putts, has one problem – he has had to alter his routine of hitting a chair leg from four feet – the reason is obvious, the repeated striking is making the chair unstable!

As for the challengers, Trevillion (the world's No. 1 putter) as was expected received many from local golfers. On this Trevillion told me: 'They could certainly knock the putts in, but when the chips were down and they were putting for high stakes they missed.'

Still undefeated, Trevillion repeats his challenge of last week to play any golfer in the world, amateur or professional, over a series of four-foot pressure putts.

One challenger who has travelled all the way down from Scotland, knocked up Trevillion at his London home and issued a direct challenge.

Trevillion was entertaining friends at the time and the challenger, Mr Willie McCrae of Glasgow, refused an offer to putt on the carpet, he demanded natural conditions.

So Trevillion motored up to his home course, Enfield, where on the sixth green he won the challenge match and was £200 richer!

During the match which lasted two putts (Trevillion holed, McCrae missed) Trevillion inadvertently interrupted a member practising to the green. To this member Trevillion extends his apologies.

We would like now to make it plain that Trevillion is not prepared to accept any more direct challenges. In future those who dispute Trevillion's claim as the world's No. 1 putter must first file their challenge through the *Golf Illustrated* offices.

As yet no professional had accepted the challenge, I was merely beating local golfers. Very few could raise the initial £1,000 stake, although one did put up a Rover Automatic. Even now I can still remember his face when I drove away in it. About this time Tom Scott, the BBC golf broadcaster, christened me 'The Messiah'. This is what he wrote as editor of *Golf Illustrated*:

By this time readers will be well aware that our valued contributor, Paul Trevillion, is both outspoken and brave. Each of his articles produce a flood of letters, some for Trevillion and some against Trevillion, for it seems you either love him or hate him.

But his claim to be the world's best putter has brought out more letters than anything else he has ever written and I understand that somehow or other readers have found out his home address and telephone number, and have also contacted him there.

Alas, I have no claim to be the world's best putter although I fancied myself pretty good on the greens at one time, but some practising in the office would seem to indicate that he has something in his new putting method. But his main theme is that his putting ideas work when a golfer is under pressure and when the rewards are high.

And whether you believe in his theories or don't believe in them you must agree that his arguments are sound, and can't be dismissed just as the thinking of some fanatic.

It could be, therefore, that Trevillion is the new golf Messiah. He certainly gets to the root of things.

Not all agreed with what he said. Ryder Cup player Brian Huggett, for instance, had some unkind things to say in the same magazine.

Trevillion is talking a lot of rubbish when he claims that he is the world's greatest putter. I don't honestly believe he has sunk a pressure putt in his life. As for the Rover car he said he won I wouldn't like to comment on that.

He mentions Paul Runyan's method of putting with a split-handed grip. Well I played with Runyan and Snead in the 1962 Open at Troon — I finished third as a matter of fact —

and in fairness Runyan holed a lot of good putts but he still missed some.

I much prefer the upright putters. People like Billy Casper, Peter Thomson and Peter Butler, who is really a fine pressure putter.

But I must admit that Bonallack putts with his chin on the green. Archer also gets well down there which underlines that putting is a very individual game and it is the method which gets the ball into the hole I recommend using.

If it has got to be a change in style I would go for the Alliss method – right hand over left. I used it myself when an assistant. I was going through a pretty bad spell on the greens at the time.

I don't believe in such an exaggerated parting of the hands as Trevillion suggests. By splitting the hands you don't get the control that you do with, say for example, the Vardon grip.

Huggett's fellow Ryder Cup man Neil Coles showed more perception:

I don't find Trevillion's putting method particularly new, in fact if I remember rightly, David Snell won the Match-play Championship with it in 1959. And then for some reason abandoned it.

I myself have never tried this, possibly because I don't think such a method would stand up against the techniques employed by such as Peter Thomson or Bobby Locke at their best.

The advantages of this method, and I'm speaking in the interest of club members who might, if in trouble, give it a try, are ... it gets your eyes right over the ball and it gives plenty of leverage in the right hand.

Trevillion's anchor-point is the left hand which he positions at the top of the club. He uses his right to swing the club through pendulum-fashion.

If I really found trouble with my putting this season I might give it a try, but I would have to be in pretty desperate straits to do it.

Finally my views are that golf is an old game, full of theories, and it seems to me the one method which has stood the test of time is the upright one.

Coles had a point here, but this was the first time the upright method for putting had received a healthy challenger. At that moment I was convinced that not only would many golfers throughout the country change to my method, they would, what's more, win with it.

Chapter 5

I Lose My Amateur Status

The inevitable happened, the Royal and Ancient Golf Club, the ruling body of golf in Britain, informed me that I had forfeited my amateur status. The reason being that I was receiving payment for the Method golf instruction I was writing in the magazine *Golf Illustrated.* My first reaction was to apply to the PGA for the necessary forms which would enable me to play the professional circuit full-time.

I did not, for one moment, imagine that I was going to win a tournament but here, I believed, was my chance to step on to a green with a well known professional and outputt him, so proving my method was superior. I knew I could outputt every pro and now I intended to prove it in front of the golfing galleries.

Unfortunately the PGA put a stop to this; they came back and informed me that I did not have the necessary credentials to join their Association. Like any other professional body, the PGA have certain rules and requirements before accepting entrants:

(1) I had to wait five years before becoming a full member of the PGA and I could only do this by qualifying at the official PGA training centre. In that five-year period I was not eligible to take part in PGA tournaments.

(2) Assistants to professionals can become full members within three years subject to qualifying at the training centre. They can then play in PGA tournaments six months after registering with the Association.

(3) To walk straight into the tournaments, as I had expected, I would, on application to the PGA, have had to have been of international standing as an amateur, recommended by the PGA Sectional Committee and be under twenty-five years of age. Six months after such an application, providing of course that I was accepted, I could have played in their tournaments.

I was now in a self-imposed golfing limbo – I could not play as an amateur, neither could I play as a professional. As a golfer, I did not exist – but the method did.

Ben Sayers, the oldest club manufacturers in the world, stepped on to the scene. It was their intention to produce an exact replica of the putter I, myself, employed. Mr P. W. Millard, their managing director, impressed me with his enthusiasm. I had no second thoughts about signing with his company. Sayers already had under contract the then reigning USPGA champion Ray Floyd and the colourful Doug Sanders. It was said in many quarters that with my signature Sayers now had golf's 'Big Three'.

I had spent a year working out the designs for the putter I used. It was centre-shafted with an all leather grip which terminated approximately eight inches from the blade. The heavy brass head had a pencil sighting mark on the top. Its overall length – thirty inches. Sayers went into production immediately, it was to be called the 'Pencil Putter'.

Four weeks after signing with Ben Sayers I received a proto-type Pencil Putter; three days later it was put to the test in a unique putting challenge match.

International show-biz star Adam Faith had just spent a five-hour session in my studio where his old putting method had been stripped away to be replaced by my split-hand method. Previously he had hit rock-bottom at Ganton. There he drove the 17th only to three-putt; then he hit two tremendous shots at the 18th to make the green and then experienced the horror of four-putting. Those seven putts on those two holes, he told me, absolutely destroyed him. Before our meeting he was seriously considering giving up the game.

Armed with my method and the proto-type Pencil Putter, Adam Faith went out and beat former Ryder Cup star Syd Scott in a tremendously exciting 18-hole impromptu challenge match at Roehampton Golf Club.

After his defeat, Syd Scott had this to say, 'On Adam Faith's efforts against me, the reports on the method have certainly not been exaggerated. When he missed a very short putt at the second I thought he had gone. It's a tribute to the method that he came back and won.'

The Ben Sayers advert which appeared in
The Golfing Press

Adam Faith

On that short missed putt, Adam had this to say, 'I thought my ball was interfering with Syd's line so I asked him if he wanted me to mark it. He nodded and made a half waving gesture with his hand. Then the thought ran through my mind that he meant me to pick it up. He was giving me the putt. But seeing that the ball was just a couple of feet from the hole I decided to stop the crosstalk and knock it in.

'I hit the ball practically on the walk and it never got near the hole. I wasn't concentrating and, worse, I had fallen back into my old putting habits. Five weeks ago such a thing would have thrown me completely, I would have three or four putted the rest of the holes. But not now – not with the Trevillion method.'

This was Syd Scott's summing up of the method that beat him, 'It will certainly help the poor putter, it certainly made Adam putt well. This splitting of the hands definitely helps to get over the "twitch"! Sam Snead with his croquet-style proved this. But the real test is, will it help the good putter?'

I was present at the challenge match and I replied, 'Of course it will help the good putter because my method contains every proven principle of good putting. Here, a self-confessed bad putter, Adam Faith, has been transformed into one good enough to beat an ex-Ryder Cup player and on the day Syd Scott did putt well. What pleased me most about Adam's performance was the way he attacked the hole. After his first two putts, both of which he left short, he was always past the hole. On this showing I can't think of any golfer, and I am including the top professionals, who could have beaten

Adam. So let's not kid ourselves, what I can do for Adam I can do for a top pro.'

By the completion of the match quite a crowd had gathered at the back of Syd Scott's pro shop. They had all been visibly impressed by what they saw and without exception they all made flattering remarks about the method.

Adam Faith summed it all up in these words, 'It was a tremendous gesture on Syd's part to play me, it just shows what a big man he is. Truth is, though, at no time did I think he would beat me. I've so much faith now in the Trevillion method – no pun intended – I expect to hole every putt and I get annoyed if I don't.

'I never lag up, I am really greedy – I want to see them all drop. During the match I knocked a really long one seven feet past, but you can do this sort of thing when you are confident of canning the return as I did. Knocking in putts like I did today was a great feeling and one I certainly never expected to experience. A lot of people said to me after the match that it was a great victory for me, but the truth is that it was a great victory for the Trevillion method.'

It was, indeed, a great victory, a convincing 3 and 1 triumph for Adam Faith, during which he holed three putts of over thirty feet.

Chapter 6

The Putter Nutter

Scores of converts were turning to the method weekly; even more encouraging, they were winning with it. One of the first to taste success was club golfer Derek Holmes, who scored his first ever Stapleford win. Not only that, it was his first win of the season and his first win in division one.

'Thanks a million, Trevillion' was his first comment. He went on, 'I have followed everything about the Trevillion method since the start. It didn't work immediately and there were times when I could have cheerfully wrapped the club round Trevillion's neck. But I persevered and the putts started dropping.

'I certainly heard some odd comments about the style, for example ... "Surely that's cheating" and "Do you want to borrow a billiard cue?" Well, my answer to all that is, when the ball's down you can stop counting.'

Holmes's winning round at the Southampton golf club included eight single putts (two thirty-footers) he had a total of twenty-nine putts in all.

John Miller (South Beds. and Royal Cinque Ports)

was another delighted winner. His success came in the Lord Brassey Challenge Cup at Deal. In winning, Miller played six rounds, of which he said, 'I have not putted better for ten years and it's all thanks to the method.' Miller, playing with Graham Clenister, also won the Halford Hewitt Medal Cup with a score of 83 less 5. The competition was played in a howling gale, which made scoring high. His partner, displeased with his putting, turned to the method half-way round with good results and said, after the round, that he putted much better after the change-over.

The trickle of winners developed into a steady flow. It was now almost impossible to count the number of converts and every bit as difficult to count the number of winners. Every section of the media – newspapers, radio and television – began to take an interest in my putting method and its achievements. I appeared on the television programme *Nationwide* where they selected the famous British astronomer, Patrick Moore OBE, a self-confessed bad putter, to put my split-hand putting method to the test. I was given thirty minutes to change Moore into a wizard on the greens.

Under the expert direction of Mark Patterson, the television cameras rolled and the experiment was captured on film. At first it looked as if Moore was a hopeless case as the first putts were well wide of the mark, but eventually the split-hand method found its groove and so did the putts. As one after the other dropped, Patrick exclaimed, 'It works!'

He went on, 'If it can work with me, whose actual handicap is somewhere in the late 70s, it must be good!'

Moore then went off to the golf course with his golfing companion, TV personality Cliff Michelmore, where he found for the first time in his golfing career that putting was easy – the Trevillion way.

Reaction was swift – over 100 telephone calls were received at the *Golf Illustrated* offices from happy viewers whose one complaint was, 'It didn't last long enough.'

Following this, a BBC national radio interview with Michael Parkinson, who at that time was one of the most respected and powerful voices in the land, provoked a wave of protest and indeed hostility. In fact even before I had left the building it hit me full blast!

'You're a putter nutter!' snarled a very elderly 'Dickensian' type gentleman, standing by the doorman. This was the same gentleman who, less than one hour before, when I had entered the building, had greeted me with a very hearty handshake, a smile and the proud boast that he had once played a round of golf with three times British Open Champion Henry Cotton.

My golfing sin which had evoked such a swift change of character was my claim that I was a better putter from four feet than Billy Casper and Arnold Palmer, two unchallengeable masters of the greens at that time.

'They are both wrist putters,' I pointed out; 'and wrist putters rely on muscle memory. They are not infallible. Furthermore, wrist putters don't last. The small muscles in the wrists break down under constant pressure. Ben Hogan and Sam Snead are proof of that fact.'

'Putter nutter', 'the nutty professor' and even 'mad-dog Trevillion' were amongst the many names coined to ridicule both myself and my method. Little did I know then that it would take nearly thirty years before it would be the generally accepted fact throughout golf that the delicate muscles of the wrists should be eliminated from the pressure action of the putting stroke.

Chapter 7

The Extended Right Arm

About this time I received a very welcome phone call from Henry Longhurst, the renowned British golf writer, television commentator and former German Amateur Champion, who served for a time as a Member of Parliament when Winston Churchill was Prime Minister.

'I'm sorry, young Paul,' he said, and I detected a note of sadness in his deep almost royal tone, 'but I feel', he sighed, 'the golf traditionalists will take a firm, unyielding and united Churchillian stand and never surrender to your method.'

Warming to the battle he carried on, 'Personally, I believe you are absolutely right. The extended right arm is indeed one of the big secrets of putting. Furthermore, I will show my colours and say as much in my column. Of course the fools will not listen, but don't you give up the fight, young Paul. Your battle, which you have fought bravely and almost single-handed, I believe is lost, but the war is still there to be won.'

I thanked Henry for the call, wished him well and then decided, at least for the time being, to leave the final putt on the method trail to be sunk by the fearless and much beloved Henry Longhurst, who that Sunday 22 March 1970 wrote at length about my split-hand putting technique. This is part of what he said:

I am sure as one reasonably can be, both from the advice of an Austrian doctor and my own personal experience which followed, that the extended right arm is one of the secrets of putting. The dreaded twitch, said my doctor friend, comes from the angle of the right elbow (he was the one who added the awful thought that 'violinists get it') and it is a demonstrable fact that even under the most severe pressure you can make a to-and-fro movement with a fully stretched right arm which you cannot with the normal putting angle. I tried this with such success that rather more than 10 years

Henry Longhurst

ago I was moved to declare that with it, if faced with a yard putt to tie for the Open, I could at any rate make some sort of stroke at the ball. I was led astray by the croquet putter and, when that went, I went too.

Even longer ago I had written about some children doing fantastic scores on our rough and ready clock golf course and this prompted a member of Lloyd's to pass on what he described as a 'sensational development of golfing science', based on the performances of an old lady with elastic-sided boots at a fete at Portmarnock. Where he and the local golfers had spent large sums of money on a 12-hole putting course before achieving a score of four under 2's, the old lady with the elastic-sided boots not only went round first time in eight under but was considerably put out on the four occasions when her first putt missed the hole.

After some months of cogitation my friend from Lloyd's hit upon the solution, namely that not only the children I had written about, one of whom would at that time have beaten the better ball of Hogan or Snead with ease – he strode after the ball as he hit it and was ready waiting at the hole side as it fell in – but also the old lady with the elastic-sided boots instinctively picked the club up, as an untaught golfer always does, with the hands wide apart.

'Everything now falls into place,' my correspondent added, 'your children, the old lady, my own vast improvement since I changed over and finally the success of the mallet-putters. Any success achieved by these diabolical weapons is due, in my opinion, not to their shape but simply to the fact that their users hold them with their hands well apart.'

Then, of course, somebody wrote to say that Harold Hilton, Open champion 1892 and 1897, Amateur champion four times, often did it too, thus proving once again that there is nothing new under the golfing sun. I suppose there is nothing for it but to get a pair of elastic-sided boots and the clubs out of the attic, extend the right arm, and start the whole ghastly business all over again.

Chapter 8

Three Wise Men

The Henry Longhurst column in the *Sunday Times* not only silenced the 'putter nutter' taunts, it had many Golf Club Secretarys, who had not only banned me from their courses but who had also insisted 'I was bringing the game of golf into disrepute' (whatever that meant!), phoning me and mumbling that there had been a misunderstanding and that I was welcome back at their clubs. Providing, of course, I did not demonstrate my split-hand putting method on their practice greens for longer than five minutes: 'it might upset some of our members, if they thought you were belittling their prowess with the traditionalist method on the green ... not the done thing, old boy!'

I always thanked them for the offer, and explained I no longer played eighteen holes of golf but I was more than prepared to pay the green fee for the use of their putting green ... usually for two hours: 'Sorry, old boy, cannot possibly agree to that' was always the swift reply. 'More than five minutes would border on an exhibition. Our members would have none of that nonsense.'

I tried to reason with them: 'But your members — those with open minds, of course — might see the merits in my method and benefit from a —'

An interruption invariably came at that juncture in my conversation, 'Merits in your method! Oh, come on now, you're not really serious? Merits! It's bending the rules. It's another version of the Sam Snead croquet style that the United States Golf Association, in its infinite wisdom, banned as illegal.'

I emphasised that my method was nothing like Sam Snead's and it was perfectly legal, but by now the voice on the other end of the line was no longer listening. 'Sorry, I'm very sorry,' it would drone on, 'but golf's a two-handed game — always has been, always will be.'

My parting line was always the same: 'If Henry Longhurst' (the name always stopped the Secretarys in their tracks even when in full verbal flow!) 'If Henry Longhurst came to your club and, as the great man has hinted, used his right arm extended down the putter shaft on your practice putting green, would he be ushered away after a five-minute warm up? ... Hello, are you still there? ...'

A slight cough and then came the reply: 'Henry Longhurst ... you are talking about one of the pillars of our golfing tradition. Now he would be a special case.'

'And myself,' I would enquire. 'Would I be a "special case" or a "nut case"?'

Another silence and the response invariably: 'I would leave you to decide that, sir!' and the phone would go dead.

Henry Longhurst was soon to be joined by two more

wise old men of golf: British Open Champions and golfing legends Max Faulkner and Henry Cotton.

In his excellent book *Play Championship Golf All Your Life*, Max Faulkner wrote,

Recently there has been a great campaign in Britain in favour of a split-handed method of putting publicised by the London artist Paul Trevillion. For short putts I am quite in favour of the two hands being apart. Holding a putter like that does away with wristiness, and if I had been younger I would have had a go at it myself, and I think I would have done well with it, for there is much to be said in its favour. But for short putts only, I fancy.

Henry Cotton said pretty much the same, insisting every golfer should give the Trevillion putting method an extensive trial.

But Henry Cotton was shaking his head gently from side to side when he put his arm round my shoulders and said: 'I'm afraid the answer is no.' He smiled and sighed, 'They do not welcome change in golf. I've suggested to two golfers who were struggling on the greens in last week's British Open to give your method a go; but I'm sorry to say, hard as I tried, they would not listen. Do you know, Paul,' he predicted, 'it will not be an Englishman or an American who will win a Major Championship with his hands well apart. They are too stubborn, too steeped in tradition. I fancy it will be a European golfer. Possibly one who has gone through all accepted methods of putting, but is still failing on the greens; who, with nowhere else to turn, and in desperation as much as anything else, will turn to your exaggerated hands-apart method and complete the stroke with his shoulders ... and, do you know, Paul, he will then go on and beat the world's best with it.'

Eighteen years were to pass before Henry Cotton's crystal-gazing prediction proved unerringly correct.

The young German Bernhard Langer had struggled with his first attack of the putting 'yips' at the start of his career when he was eighteen years old. He battled on for some years before changing to the 'cross-handed' method. This proved successful. It appeared he had conquered the 'yips' once and for all.

Unfortunately Langer's stroke began to tighten up. His wrists began to over-react and his putting stroke broke down at the 1988 British Open Championship at Royal Lytham and St Annes, when he five-putted the 17th green on his way to an 80!

It was one of the saddest sights I had witnessed on a putting green. This talented young golfer looked a broken man and the generally accepted opinion in golf was that the German who had tried everything in search of a cure for the putting 'yips' was finished ... his career over.

Chapter 9

A Sure Way of Beating the Putting Trembles

Dear Sir,

Mr Trevillion states he is the best putter in the world and he may be right. My golf pals insist I am the best putter in the world. I agree I don't win very often but this is simply because my long game is so bad.

My technique is very simple. I place the putter in my left hand only. I then rest the putter head on the ground as close as possible to the ball with the blade meticulously at right angles to the line of flight. Leaving the putter head completely at rest I then move quietly behind the ball and with my right foot I give the back of the putter head a gentle kick.

I must say I expect the ball to go straight into the hole.

Dr Garfield Evans,
127, Cathedral Road,
Cardiff

On receiving the above letter, which I've quoted already in the Introduction, my first reaction was to ask Dr Garfield what make of football boots he recommended for kicking the putts home. As his letter suggested the doctor had a sense of humour. 'Suit yourself,' he laughed, 'and then give the method a try; it works.'

Having said that the laughter vanished from the doctor's voice. 'I have, indeed, kicked putts in this way,' he went on, 'but only to prove the point that the larger muscles in the body, the leg muscles in this case, can withstand pressure to a far greater degree than the smaller muscles in the body.

'Notice when a person gets nervous how it is the hands that are the first to tremble. It is the small muscles in the body which are the most susceptible to pressure when tension mounts. The larger muscles can withstand pressure, it needs an almighty shock, far bigger than one would normally experience in golf, to get a man shaking from head to foot.'

Dr Garfield, eighty-seven years of age, has seen most of the world's top golfers – Bobby Jones, James Braid, J. H. Taylor, in action. 'I agree, your Trevillion putting method can, indeed, help off-set the dreaded "yips",' he

Bob Charles

went on. 'Successful putting depends on how well you react under pressure because it is pressure — tension, if you like — which determines the fate of the putt. This, of course, is what makes your method so sound under pressure. Your right shoulder being the axis for the putting stroke, means you use the whole of the right arm from the shoulder to the finger-tips in the putting stroke. It is this almost straight right arm which helps you to resist the tensions experienced when facing a pressure putt of four feet and under.

'This, again, is why Bob Charles is such a great putter: he uses his shoulders. I have even heard it said that a golfer should employ the hips when he putts, moving them from side to side with the big thigh muscles doing the work.

'A wrist putter will, indeed, be more liable to suffer from the shakes because the delicate muscles in the hands and wrists cannot withstand the build-up of pressure so easily. For beating tension on the green, I would say your Trevillion putting method is ideal.'

Chapter 10

The Reason for Splitting the Hands

In everyday life the left and right hands rarely work as one unit. In general the left hand steadies while the right hand goes to work – knotting a tie; putting your coat on (it's always your right arm you put in first); working with a garden spade; pressing a stubborn toothpaste tube; tying a shoe lace and so on. The moment the left hand has to work with the right, people will say, 'I'm all fingers and thumbs today.' This is because the left hand is hindering not helping, it is performing an unnatural role and subconsciously your mind rebels against this.

The same goes for putting – on your week-end round you try to get the left and the right hand to work as one unit. You're asking them to adopt an unfamiliar relationship, a relationship which has not been asked of them since the last week-end you played.

What happens? The left hand becomes stubborn, it resists and restricts the working of the right hand at impact, the putt is pulled or pushed to one side of the hole. Even the world's top professionals will remark after a bad round of putting, 'I had no feel in my hands

49

today,' but this is an inaccurate statement, what they should have said was, 'my left hand was not co-operating.' Your right hand will always react the same, day in and day out. I've never seen or heard of a person attempting to cut a piece of steak remark, 'I just can't keep it on the plate, I have no feel in my hands today.'

The reason Orville Moody, a self-confessed bad putter, found success when he adopted the cack-handed grip (right over left) is because when the left hand is in this position it has no function other than to hold the club, the right hand has to do the work.

This is why those elderly gentlemen on bowling greens show no signs of the 'yips'. You can watch them Sunday after Sunday rolling the bowl up with their right hand with no semblance of a shake, and why should there be?

Your right hand is constantly working for you, performing the most difficult tasks, it sees no problems in knocking a putt in the hole. It's just as simple as asking it to undo a button.

A wealthy man I knew, who played a lot of golf and employed a split-handed grip, once told me something I've never forgotten. Taking from his wallet a handful of notes he said to me, 'Money, no matter how much you've got, is a very precious commodity, and people do not like to make mistakes with such a valuable commodity. This is why they hold the notes with the LEFT HAND and count each one with the RIGHT. The right hand is your BUSINESS HAND; rely on it and it will never let you down.'

Walter Travis, whose many remarkable putting feats

gave him a healthy claim to the title 'the greatest putter that ever lived', had this to say on the subject in the book *Great Golfers in the Making*.

'I believe that putting should be done always with one hand – with one hand actively at work, that is. The left hand should be used only for the purpose of swinging the clubhead backwards preparatory to making the stroke. When it has done that its work is done, and the right hand should then be the sole master of the situation, the left being merely kept in attachment to it for steadying purposes. WHEN ONLY ONE HAND IS THUS EMPLOYED THE GAIN IN ACCURACY IS VERY GREAT. Two hands at work on a short putt or a long one tend to distraction. When the stroke is being made the grip of the right hand should be firm, but not tight, and after impact the clubhead should be allowed to pass clean through with an easy following stroke. The follow-through should indeed be as long as possible to make it comfortably and with this object in view, at the moment of touching the ball THE GRIP OF THE FINGERS OF THE LEFT HAND SHOULD BE CONSIDERABLY RELAXED SO THAT THE RIGHT HAND MAY GO ON DOING ITS WORK WITHOUT INTERRUPTION.'

Which leads on to the question, did Vardon hinder or help? Golf, cricket, baseball, hockey, hurling, lacrosse and ice-hockey are all two-handed sports. Of these, golf is the only one in which the hands are overlapped on the grip. Is it right to believe that all these other sports are the ones out of step? Before you make a snap decision I advise you to read on for I have explained in full the opinion expressed by Mr H. H. Hilton, who played in those historic days when the overlap grip was pioneered.

The big six golfers in those days of gutty balls, wooden cleeks and bumpy greens, were Harry Vardon, J. H. Taylor, James Braid, Alex Herd, Mr H. H. Hilton and Mr John Ball, Jr. Of these Vardon, Taylor and Braid employed the overlapping grip, the other three employed what is known today as the baseball grip, every finger on the club.

It is interesting to recall that the three who used the overlapping grip – Vardon, Taylor and Braid – used a great deal of wrist-work in the stroke. By employing the overlapping grip they ensured the bringing of the hands close together so allowing both wrists to work in unison.

On the theory of the overlapping grip, Mr Harold H. Hilton – incidentally, the only amateur to win the Open Championship twice and a former editor of *Golf Illustrated* – had this to say. 'Providing you are sufficiently powerful in the hands, try the overlapping grip for it enables the wrists to work together.' Hilton, an extremely small man in stature, standing no more than 5' 6" in height, then added this warning and in doing so underlined why he, a man with average-sized hands, employed the baseball grip. 'I have found that to work the overlapping grip successfully, the golfer must, of necessity, have very long and powerful fingers. For if he has not there is far too much strain placed upon the left hand and wrist and the right hand (three fingers only on the club) does not have a sufficiently firm grip of the club to apply to requisite power.'

With those words, Hilton explained why my split-

The two-handed grip

hand putting technique is the only way to putt. The one thing every golfer agrees on where putting is concerned is that it is a right-handed stroke, so now let's analyse Hilton's remark and check what happens when a golfer mistakenly putts with the overlap grip:

1. He considerably weakens the master right hand.
2. Both wrists have to work in unison.
3. A simple one-handed strike is turned into a complicated two-handed action.

THE TREVILLION METHOD

With my split-handed putting method, the left hand serves but one purpose, it anchors the club position. Now the right hand is free to do its job – UNHINDERED by the left. The stroke now becomes one of simplicity; the right hand, with all fingers on the club, assumes complete authority over the striking action.

I can think of no other sport where fellow professionals check each other's grip – which, to my way of thinking, leads me to believe that over-emphasis on the Vardon grip has HINDERED as much as it has helped golf, especially PUTTING.

THE PENCIL PUTT TEST

When putting, the secret is to take the putter straight back and through – an extremely difficult thing to do if you adopt the Vardon overlap grip. You can prove this for yourself by holding a pencil in your normal putting grip and then drawing a line. It will, I assure you, be far from straight. Now hold the pencil in just your right

The Vardon grip

hand (providing you are right-handed) and draw another line under the one which you have just completed. You will, I promise, be surprised just how much straighter the second line is.

Chapter 11

The Truth about the Cross-Hand Putting Method

When a golfer as technically correct as South African Gary Player openly admits that he has been using the wrong putting grip since he started golf, the time has come when every deep-thinking golfer must seriously consider if he is using the correct grip.

At the time of writing, Player, desperately seeking a cure, was experimenting with the cross-handed putting grip, insisting that it was not a panic measure but the result of a lot of thought. For Player's information I can prove, without fear of contradiction, that this will only lead to a temporary cure. Player is literally driving down a one-way street in the wrong direction – he will eventually have to stop, reverse and start again.

In that excellent book – *Golf's Winning Stroke – Putting* we find the following:

The cross-handed putting grip began to enjoy a considerable vogue about 1965. Fred Haas, Jr, the veteran New Orleans professional who became the United States Seniors Champion in 1965, had been using the technique for several years. It was subsequently adopted by such successful pros as Johnny

Johnny Pott

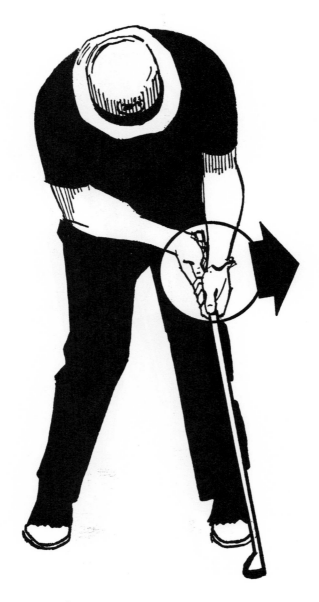

Orville Moody

Pott, Wes Ellis, Jr, Jim Ferree, Peter Alliss and among the ladies, Marilyn Smith. As its name implies, the essential feature of this grip is that the hands are crossed. There are minor variations of this grip. Ellis describes his own – 'My grip is the interlocking with the little finger of my left hand twining round the fore-finger of my right hand. I putt right-handed, the back of my left hand and the palm of my right hand face towards the hole. My thumbs are directly on top of the shaft. The face of the putter remains square to the line for a longer time without any special effort on my part to keep it square.'

Johnny Pott went so far as to have a specially manufactured putter grip with a flat top. This enabled him to place both thumbs on the flat surface and for him it helped considerably. As it was, both Ellis and Pott proved better than average putters with the cross-handed method.

In 1969 Orville Moody exploded on to the golf scene when he won the US Open putting cross-handed. Said Orville at the time:

'The reason I switched was because I developed a case of the "yips". I'd yip one left of the hole and then on the next putt, I'd try not to do that and I'd leave it on the other side. I putted so poorly I just had to do something.'

Orville described his technique thus – 'I placed the right hand up high on the grip. The left hand is placed directly below the right, but with all my fingers on the shaft – no overlapping.' (This is an improvement on the Pott–Ellis method where overlapping and interlocking was employed.) 'Putting has always been a right-handed action for me and this method helps me to keep the ball on line. A one-piece arm motion ensures that the wrists remain firm.'

In the golf magazine *Golf Monthly*, their renowned contributor, Mr X. has this to say on the cross-handed grip:

It works because it keeps the shoulders level at address, while the orthodox putting grip tends to raise the left shoulder and lower the right. But when the left shoulder is higher than the right at address and there is any shoulder movement during the putt then the left shoulder tends to turn away from the line, causing the putt to be cut.

From what I have said readers will note that the main advantages for the cross-handed method of putting are:

(a) it keeps the shoulders level at address,
(b) it allows the right hand to execute the stroke,
(c) there is a much firmer anchor point as the left hand is nearer the putter blade.
(d) When the shoulders are level at address then the left shoulder can RISE (during the putting action) without turning.

These are the advantages, but the one drawback which has retarded the growth of this method since 1965 (only a minority use it – Player, please note) is that, even with the Orville Moody ten-finger grip, the left hand hinders rather than helps.

Without labouring the advantages of my split-hand method, I feel I should make it clear now just why this technique is the only 100 per cent successful method. In the drawing you can see that at address my right and

left hands are at the same level, this ensures my shoulders also being at the same level. I then bend my left arm to anchor the club at the top. I now place my right hand on the shaft and I can, with no restrictions from my left hand, produce the ultimate in putting – AN UNHINDERED RIGHT-HAND STROKE.

As long as I keep my right palm facing the hole, back and through the stroke, there is absolutely no way I can miss a putt of four feet and under and the six thousand converts who have turned to the split-hand method will confirm this.

Part Two

THE MECHANICS OF THE METHOD

'The only people who will criticise the Trevillion split-hand putting method are those unable to analyse it for themselves. I, myself, have analysed it and found it contains the proven principles of putting.'
TOM BOVINGDON – Golf professional

Chapter 12
Feel

Feel is the biggest misconception in putting. It's nonsense to say, and many great putters do, that you must hold the club no tighter than when feeling your own pulse.

To say you must feel the grip in your hand for 'touch' when putting, I repeat, is a total *misconception*.

You can check this out for yourself when building with cards, coins or whatever; the higher you get, the more delicately you try to place the next one on top and, eventually, it's your shaking, unsteady hand that topples the lot.

Ninety per cent of golfers take the wrists out of the putting action, but then they subconsciously reintroduce them when they strive for feel when gripping the club.

You should instead hold your putter tightly enough to ensure you feel the putter head strike the ball. The same way an artist only feels the pencil point on the paper. He is totally unaware of holding the pencil.

The truth is, it's impossible to pull a pencil from the finger and thumb of an artist, so strong and positive is

Renoir

his grip when drawing. In short the grip is *tight* but never *tense*.

Don't take my word for it. The great French master Renoir, helpless in his old age, crippled with arthritis and twisted joints, considered himself a lucky man because he was able to paint in his bath chair with the brush bound tightly to his wrist with rolls of sticking tape. Renoir called it 'putting on his thumb'. The Renoir brush strokes transferred to canvas in this manner seemed to gain in youth and energy.

Renoir accepted that he could no longer sculpt, but by directing the hands of two young artists by means of a long stick strapped to his wrist, like a magic wand, he

Bernhard Langer

conjured up a massive sculpture of a young goddess of breathtaking beauty.

The struggle of the crippled artist is one of the heroic legends of art.

Today Bernhard Langer grips the club with his left hand well down the shaft, then uses his right hand to strap the putter to his left arm. Then, like Renoir, he draws a straight line to the hole and invariably the putt drops in.

Chapter 13

Straight Back – Straight Through

On short putts, the putter blade must be taken *straight back* and *straight through* to the hole.

For those who say the putter blade must be taken back slightly *inside* the line then straightened up again in line with the hole on impact with the ball, I say think again.

To deliberately take the putter blade off line once you have painstakingly lined it up is madness. You are relying on muscle memory to straighten it up again and nobody is that good. More short putts are missed in this manner than in any other way.

Secondly, the blade must travel low to the ground back and through the stroke to ensure impact on the centre of the ball. This produces a true roll. The ball is round; if struck correctly in this manner the ball will hug the ground and keep its line.

If the blade lifts when you make contact with the ball on your follow-through, you will impart too much overspin and the ball will roll with less control.

If you lift the blade on the backswing, chances are

you will make contact with the ball with a downwards strike and impart excess backspin and the ball will finish short of the hole.

Chapter 14

Never Be Short

No golfer has suffered more on the greens than the 'voice of golf', Peter Alliss, which is why I have never met anyone who speaks with more authority or sense on the art of getting the ball into the hole.

It was Alliss who told me that, as long as I lived, I would never find a hole that would come up and meet the ball – the ball must go to the hole. Alliss also believed, and rightly so, that the golfer who misses his putts by going past the hole is an infinitely better putter than the player who misses his by always being short.

The player who is always finishing six inches short very seldom three-putts, but then he will hardly, if ever, one-putt. Whereas the player who is always going past the hole gets a great number of single putts. Yes, he may also get a couple of threes, but if you don't get your share of one-putts you are not going to win a Championship.

The greatest pressure-putter in the history of golf was undoubtedly Arnold Palmer.

Arnold thought nothing of charging the first putt four

feet past the hole. The return, he considered, was a simple tap-in.

I think American Doug Ford, winner of the Masters and a great pressure-putter, summed it up best when he said: 'I was never short with my first, second, third, fourth or fifth putt!'

So there you have it. Be brave ... go for the hole and knock it in. There is no other way to win a Championship.

Chapter 15

The Putting Greats

I have spent almost thirty years researching and analysing the great putters who have dominated Championship golf. My special heroes all come from a similar mould, preach pretty much the same techniques and sank most of those all-important four-footers.

If you study my method you will find it contains all the proven principles that these great men moulded into their Championship-winning putting stroke.

HARRY VARDON – STOOPED TO CONQUER

All the early golfing greats – Harry Vardon, Walter J. Travis, Walter Hagen, Gene Sarazen – got well down to their work. They were all confirmed crouchers over the ball.

The centre or axis of the putting stroke is the top of the spine between the shoulder blades.

In a crouched position using this axis, the shoulders, arms and hands move in a parallel line with the green.

If anyone knows of a better human support for a

Harry Vardon

pendulum, he should immediately inform the medical council.

Slamming Sam Snead was a dynamic wrist putter. He had to be, to have won over 100 tournaments.

Then in 1966 at the Firestone Club in Akron, Ohio, Sam set up short birdie putts on the first nine holes and missed the lot.

On the 10th hole Sam straddled the line and, croquet-style, rattled the putts in.

The US Golf Association banned it as illegal.

Sam changed to side saddle. Hinging the club at the top of the grip, Sam used the shoulder and the whole arm with the wrist of the moving arm taken out of the stroke.

Sam cleaned up on the Seniors tour, and he's still winning today.

Sam Snead

BOB CHARLES — THE PENDULUM

Bob Charles is still the finest left-handed putter in the game.

Charles favours the square method of putting. Hands parallel to each other, shoulders, hips, feet in line with the hole. Putter blade in line with the hole.

Charles takes the putter straight back and straight

Bob Charles

through. His shoulders moving in a vertical plane, creating the perfect pendulum action.

Every inch you raise the head above the horizontal tilts the axis of the swing and introduces inaccuracies.

ARNOLD PALMER — POWER PUTTER

The most confident, positive and attacking putter of my time was Arnold Palmer.

He thought nothing of banging the ball four feet past. The return distance was a tap-in.

Most short putts are missed due to the failure to follow-through. This is caused by fear of being too firm.

Yet firmness is demanded even in the shortest of strokes.

Arnold Palmer

There are those who say the follow-through has no effect whatsoever on what happens to the ball once it has left the club face.

Nonsense – this is where the confidence of the golfer is exposed.

A confident follow-through makes the putt. It's a clear indication of what went on before the ball left the club face.

You must take the putter face to the hole.

JACK NICKLAUS – FREEZE FRAME

Jack Nicklaus bends low over the ball in a crouched position.

Jack holds his putter almost vertical at address to

Jack Nicklaus

ensure he swings the club pendulum-like, with the putter face on line to the hole throughout the stroke.

Jack holds his breath, as if he's frozen in ice throughout the stroke. It allows his body to remain still and only his arms to make the stroke.

Nobody in the history of golf has played the pressure putts better.

LEE TREVINO — TEN-FINGER GRIP

The name of the game is getting the ball in the hole and no golfer does it better than Lee Trevino.

I remember Lee telling me he placed all ten fingers on the grip by sliding his right hand down the grip a fraction. This gave him the feeling of having more control with his right hand. Then, by placing both of his thumbs pointing straight down the shaft, he had both palms facing and this kept the wrists out of action as much as possible.

With the hands in this position Lee believed he prevented pushing or pulling a putt and he was dead right.

Trevino never faces a pressure putt, because with his method there is no pressure.

Lee Trevino

SAM TORRANCE — BROOM HANDLE

Sam Torrance popularised the Broom Handle technique, but the critics say putting should be about feel and the Broom Handle is nothing more than a mechanical action. Nonsense. Short putts have nothing to do with feel. It's about swinging the club like a pendulum.

Sam Torrance

Torrance hinges the club at his chin. The left hand and arm have no place in the stroke, except to anchor the top of the handle to the chin.

The right hand holds the club like a pencil and the putter blade is directed along the line of the putt by the whole of the right arm.

BERNHARD LANGER — THE MECHANIC

The Langer method is technically the Broom Handle stroke in miniature.

Langer grips the club with his left hand then uses his right hand to clamp the putter to his left arm. The clamp prevents the left wrist from breaking down.

Bernhard Langer

As with the Broom Handle, the action requires a large shoulder movement for even the shortest putt.

In short, it's a small stroke controlled by the big muscles.

Chapter 16

One-Putt Knock-In

There is one sketch missing from my collection of putting greats. That's because he's not a golfer. He was a fighter. Possibly the greatest fighter pound for pound who ever lived.

His name was Sugar Ray Robinson and he is the one man above all others who I have to thank for my 'one-punch knock-out', or, to put it in golfing terms, my 'one-putt knock-in'!

The year was 1951. I was a schoolboy and Sugar Ray Robinson was the Middleweight Champion of the World. He had come to England to fight Britain's Randolph Turpin. I had done a drawing of Robinson and my local newspaper arranged for me to meet the great man.

As he autographed my sketch he looked up and said, 'When I was your age I was tap-dancing on the sidewalks of New York and I was doing pretty good.'

I asked him what made a champion. He said one word, '*Balance*'.

He then walked towards me, stopped and said, 'Look at the position of my feet. The width they are apart, with my normal walking stride, which I have been rehearsing for a lifetime I might add, gives me my *stance* for perfect body balance. With my feet in this position I can, if I bend my knees and come up on my toes, dance like a ballerina or, if I drop my heels and stand flat footed, I can from that position punch my full weight and hit with the power of a heavyweight. Now remember, you hit from the shoulder and connect with your fist. Then it's lights out, good night, your opponent's history. I repeat, you hit from the shoulder and connect with your fist. Then it's lights out, good night, your opponent's history. Never forget it.'

I never did forget and that's the secret of my *one-putt knock-in*.

I hit from the shoulder and connect with my putter blade. Then it's lights out, good night ... the *putt's history!*

Chapter 17

The Perfect Putting Method

I will now talk you through the thinking behind my *one-putt knock-in.*

1. The Putting Stance

As Sugar Ray Robinson said, the width your feet are apart with your natural walking stride is the perfect platform for your body weight. So that is your putting stance. Check it out: drop a ball on the floor and walk up to it. Stop and now bend your knees and you are as solid and as steady as a rock.

No body or head movement throughout the arms and club-putting stroke.

2. The Putting Crouch

I tilt from the waist and ensure my shoulders are parallel to the ground. The centre or axis of the putting stroke is the top of the spine between the shoulder blades. You could place a tray across my back and balance a drinking-glass on top and the liquid inside the glass would be perfectly level.

3. The Soling of the Putter

I have the sole of my putter perfectly level with the ground. I start my putting stroke by lifting it slightly, to ensure I do not catch the grass on the backswing and follow-through.

4. Eyes Over the Ball

My eyes are directly over the ball. You can check this out by dropping a ball from the bridge of your nose. It should land on the ball below.

5. *Alignment to the Hole – The Square Method*

With all short putts the ball must be hit firmly enough to eliminate any borrow along a straight line to the hole. Having decided on your line to the hole, your putter

club-face and body must be positioned along this line square to the hole. This is known as 'The Square Method'. Your feet, ankles, knees, hips and shoulders are in line with the hole.

6. Grip Pressure

My grip is tight, just like I hold a pencil; but it is never *tense*. I repeat, *never tense*. Forget 'feel' for the short putt. The ball is too close to the hole for 'feel' to play any part.

Don't just take my word for it, check it out. Palmer aside, the two greatest pressure-putters of all time, Jack Nicklaus and Lee Trevino, putt with their gloves on. Now, if you wanted maximum 'feel', wouldn't it be smart to putt with the glove off?

So, I repeat, forget 'feel' when it comes to the short putt.

7. My Grip Secret

Now I'm going to tell you about my grip secret. If you check out the drawing of my left fist you will see four knuckles.

Now check out the drawing of my right fist ... and you will notice only three knuckles are prominent. I lost my left little finger knuckle – a compound fracture – demonstrating the Sugar Ray Robinson knock-out punch! This caused a major problem when I tried to draw a straight line. My hand rolled over, pulling the middle knuckle of my right fore-finger out of line. For the first time in my life my drawing line was no longer true. A trip to the hospital, another x-ray and the

specialist arranged for me to have a surgical pad fitted where my little finger knuckle used to be to keep my right fore-finger middle knuckle on top of the pencil. It worked. I was back drawing a straight line again.

It's the same when putting. The middle knuckle of the right fore-finger must point centrally between the toes. If the middle knuckle of the right fore-finger points slightly to your right toe, you push the putt wide of the hole. If the middle knuckle of the right fore-finger points slightly to your left toe, you pull the putt wide of the hole.

I have taken the positioning of the right fore-finger out of the putting stroke by placing it behind the putter-shaft. This helps direct my right palm to the hole.

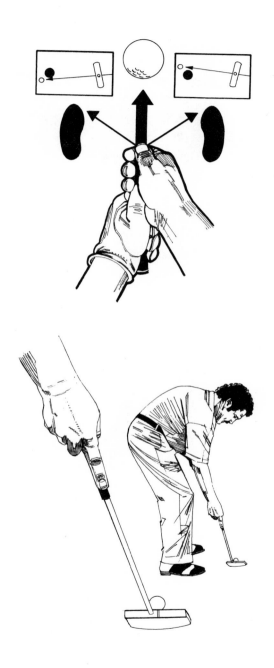

8. The Pendulum Stroke

Both my arms hang naturally from the shoulders with both palms of my hands facing each other and perfectly level with each other. Because I want to take my right palm to the hole pendulum-fashion, I take my left hand out of the stroke by placing it at the top of the grip. Using my right shoulder I take the club straight back and through.

9. The Strike

As a mental image I imagine the ball is asleep. I give it a hard whack, its eyes open ... it sees the hole and it dives in. The putt's history!

10. The Follow-Through

A confident follow-through sinks the putt. It's a clear indication of what went on before you struck the ball. You must take the putter face to the hole.

Chapter 18

Why Four Feet?

The question I'm most asked is 'why four feet?'

Firstly, from that distance the borrow doesn't decide the fate of the putt. If the ball is hit hard enough it will take out any borrow even on a fast green with a downhill left-to-right putt. Secondly, I'll take you back to Muirfield, the year is 1972 and it's the 17th hole of the final round of the British Open. Lee Trevino is in the rough and Tony Jacklin is on the green. Trevino from the rough chips in and from four feet Jacklin three-putts!

Trevino won the 1972 British Open and Jacklin, who up to that time could putt the eyes out of a squirrel, was never a serious contender for the Major Championships again.

There are hundreds of great putters – too many for me to mention who have been broken and destroyed from the four-foot area. They know they shouldn't miss, but they do. That is why my split-hand method, twenty-five years on, is now becoming fashionable.

Nevertheless, there are still many traditionalists and

'doubting Thomases' who challenge my method ... they call it a 'gimmick'.

In the same way Johnny 'Tarzan' Weissmuller, who was never beaten in over 100 swimming races and who won a bucketful of Olympic Golds with his revolutionary front-crawl whiplash leg action – he used each leg as a whip and his feet as a lash, propelling himself forward with unbelievable power – was told his method was a 'gimmick'.

In the 1968 Olympics, Bob Fosbury revolutionised the High Jump with his backward leap ... They called his method a 'gimmick'.

In the early 1970s USA's Jimmy Connors introduced the two-handed backhand return. They laughed and said 'it's fine for the ladies like Chris Evert because they are the weaker sex.'

Once again they called it a 'gimmick'.

I will tell you the definition of a 'gimmick'. It's something you wished you had thought of first. Which is so sad, especially when I think back to 1968.

The place was my house. It was there that I showed Peter Alliss, TV's Mr Golf, my putting method.

A ball was placed on the carpet four feet from the leg of a chair and, with Alliss watching, I hit that chair leg with six consecutive putts using my split-hand method.

Alliss adopted the method and repeated the feat, but with a difference. Each of his strikes were so true the ball rolled back to him, where as the majority of mine had bounced off at different angles.

Three days later, I saw Peter on the Stoke Poges

practice putting green. I asked him if he was experimenting with my method. He gave a practical answer ... he separated his grip and knocked in three four-footers.

'Are you going to use it in the tournament?' I asked.

He shook his head. 'I have a tough enough job explaining how I miss with the conventional method. I'd be lost for words using your method.'

Alliss finished second in the tournament to Clive Clark, but had he used my method he would have won. He missed four putts of under four feet.

Alliss was the one man I feared in those days. He was a better putter with my method than Bernhard Langer is today.

I have no doubts that if Peter Alliss had adopted my method he would have won a lot of Majors. He was that good a golfer.

The first golfer to have the moral courage to adopt my method to improve his putting when he is already a good putter will be perfection on the greens.

I'm not a golfer, I don't profess to having much of a game, but I am an artist who can draw a straight line on a green ... and, from four feet, I can beat any man in the world.

Chapter 19

Questions Answered

P. French, Newquay, Cornwall
'Being a little overweight I find it extremely difficult
when bending from the waist as your method demands.
Have you an alternative suggestion for getting down
over the ball?'

FOR THOSE WHO WANT TO GET DOWN OVER THE
BALL WITHOUT EXCESSIVE BENDING, COPY BERNARD
DARWIN IN THE ILLUSTRATION, AND SIMPLY WIDEN
YOUR STANCE. THIS WILL, INDEED, BRING YOU DOWN
AS FAR AS REQUIRED.

T. Thatcher, Sidcup, Kent
'At address does the weight favour one foot in par-
ticular?'

NO, THE WEIGHT IS EVENLY DISTRIBUTED ON EACH
FOOT GIVING CENTRAL CONTROL AND ELIMINATING
BODY SWAY.

R. Morgan, Tavistock, Devon
'Can you tell me the exact position for the ball at address?'

I, PERSONALLY, FIND THAT THE BEST RESULTS ARE OBTAINED WHEN THE BALL IS POSITIONED AN INCH OFF THE CENTRE OF MY STANCE IN THE DIRECTION OF MY LEFT TOE. THIS WAY THE RIGHT ARM CAN SWING IN PENDULUM FASHION, ALLOWING THE CLUB-HEAD TO STRIKE THE BALL AT THE BOTTOM OF ITS SWING ARC.

E. Woodley, Romsey, Hants
'I have noticed that you recommend the putter should be taken straight back and straight through for putts of four feet and under. But what about putts that exceed this length. Is the principle the same?'

FOR PUTTS OF FOUR FEET AND UNDER THE PUTTER MUST BE TAKEN STRAIGHT BACK AND STRAIGHT THROUGH. BUT FOR ANYTHING OVER THAT LENGTH, TAKE THE PUTTER BLADE BACK SLIGHTLY INSIDE THE LINE. IF YOU TOOK THE PUTTER BLADE STRAIGHT BACK ON A LONG PUTT OF, SAY, THIRTY FEET, THERE WOULD BE A TENDENCY TO LIFT IT TOO HIGH OFF THE GROUND.

S. Salmon, Guildford, Surrey
'Do you break the right wrist when you take the putter back?'

NO, WHEN I SWING THE CLUBHEAD BACK, THE RIGHT WRIST REMAINS FIRM. THE AXIS IS THE RIGHT SHOULDER, ALLOWING THE PUTTER BLADE TO BRUSH THE GRASS ON THE BACKSWING AND CONTINUE TO BRUSH THE GRASS AT IMPACT AND INTO THE FIRST STAGE OF THE FOLLOW THROUGH.

T. Hardy, Pontypridd, Glamorgan
'No matter how straight you hit a putt, it will only drop if you line it up correctly. Obviously you have no trouble here but I am afraid I do. If you have a tip which could help me, I would be pleased to hear of it.'

WHEN I LINE UP A PUTT ON THE GREEN I ADOPT THE SAME PRINCIPLES AS USED WHEN LINING UP A TEE SHOT. IN OTHER WORDS, I STAND BEHIND THE BALL AND PLACE THE PUTTER AT RIGHT ANGLES TO THE

HOLE. THEN, HOLDING THE PUTTER IN THIS POSITION IN MY LEFT HAND, I MOVE ROUND AND ADOPT MY NORMAL PUTTING STANCE.

R. Pickard, London, Middlesex
'Can I use your method of putting for short chip shots just off the green?'

YES INDEED, I MYSELF HAVE TRIED IT WITH EXCEL-LENT RESULTS.

D. Bailey, Fleetwood, Lancashire
'Is it necessary to have the right forefinger down the back of the shaft?'

YES. YOUR RIGHT HAND IS THE MASTER HAND, IT KNOCKS THE PUTTS IN. THE MORE CONTACT THIS HAND HAS WITH THE CLUB, THE MORE CONTROL YOU HAVE OVER THE STRIKE.

Mrs J. Hill, Worthing, Sussex
'I think I am taking the putter straight back and through to the hole, but I am not absolutely certain. Nor is my playing partner. Is there an easy way I can check this?'

YES, PRACTISE A FEW PUTTS ON YOUR LIVING-ROOM CARPET, CLOSE TO THE SKIRTING-BOARD. ANY DEVI-ATION WILL THEN BE QUICKLY SPOTTED.

Trevillion Punch Putter

M. Wilson, Glasgow, Scotland
'I have cut six inches off my putter and find the method works to a degree. Unfortunately I do not feel so confident when handling my putter at its reduced size.'

THIS IS UNDERSTANDABLE FOR YOU HAVE, BY CUTTING THE SHAFT, DESTROYED THE CLUB'S BALANCE. I AM AGAINST CUTTING DOWN A STANDARD-LENGTH PUTTER FOR IT INVARIABLY PROVES UNSATISFACTORY.

This is one of the reasons why I was delighted Golfstyx in England and The Booklegger in the USA placed my Trevillion Punch Putter on the market. This two-grip putter is standard length, enabling you to putt in the traditional manner until you are within the four-foot pressure zone. Then you can split your grip by placing your right hand down onto the lower grip. In this position it's easy to direct your right palm to the hole and sink the pressure putt.